Give a man a fish, and you feed him for a day. Teach a man to fish, and you feed him for a lifetime.

Anne Isabella Thackeray Ritchie

50 YEARS OF STRENGTHENING OUR COMMUNITY

50th ANNIVERSARY

STARGROUP
INTERNATIONAL

50 YEARS OF STRENGTHENING OUR COMMUNITY

50th ANNIVERSARY

Goodwill
Gulfstream Goodwill Industries

StarGroup International, Inc. West Palm Beach, Florida

Concept & supervision: Brenda Star

Project coordinator: Brian Edwards

Book and cover design: Mel Abfier

Senior Editor: Jessica Winter

Editorial Assistant: Rebeca Krogman

Designed and produced by StarGroup International, Inc.

(561) 547-0667
www.stargroupinternational.com

Gulfstream Goodwill Industries
www.gulfstreamgoodwill.org

Printed in Canada

Library of Congress Cataloging-in-Publication 2015955185

50th Anniversary - 50 YEARS OF STRENGTHENING OUR COMMUNITY

ISBN 978-1-884886-19-5

table of contents

MISSION

Gulfstream Goodwill Industries Mission

Gulfstream Goodwill Industries assists people with disabilities and other barriers to employment to become self-sufficient, working members of our community.

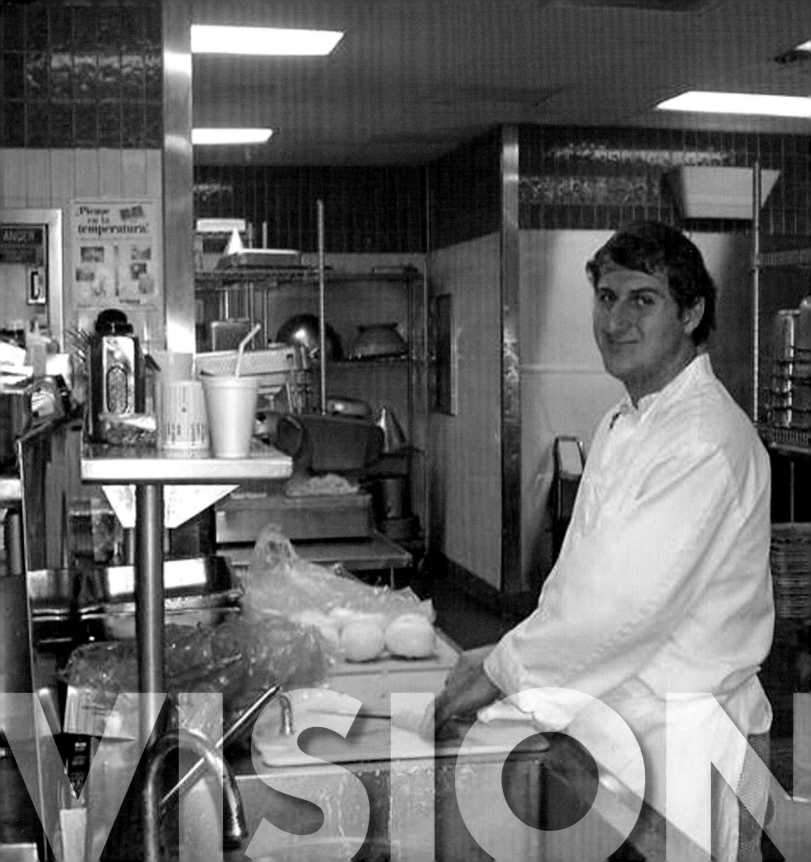

Gulfstream Goodwill Industries Vision

We will be the premier provider of quality rehabilitation, education, employment, and training opportunities for people with barriers to employment and independence.

BOARD
LEADERSHIP

THEN ...

M.P. "HAM" ANTHONY
FOUNDER AND FORMER MAYOR OF WEST PALM BEACH
1966

... NOW

BERT PREMUROSO
IMMEDIATE PAST CHAIRPERSON OF
THE BOARD OF DIRECTORS
2016

DENISE McDONALD
CHAIRPERSON OF THE BOARD OF DIRECTORS
2016

50th ANNIVERSARY

THE JOB

Jobs provide individuals with a sense of purpose and personal fulfillment. They provide the opportunity to contribute to the evolution of organizational culture, while building autonomy. These are the intangible benefits of work.

Commission on Accreditation of Rehabilitation Facilities

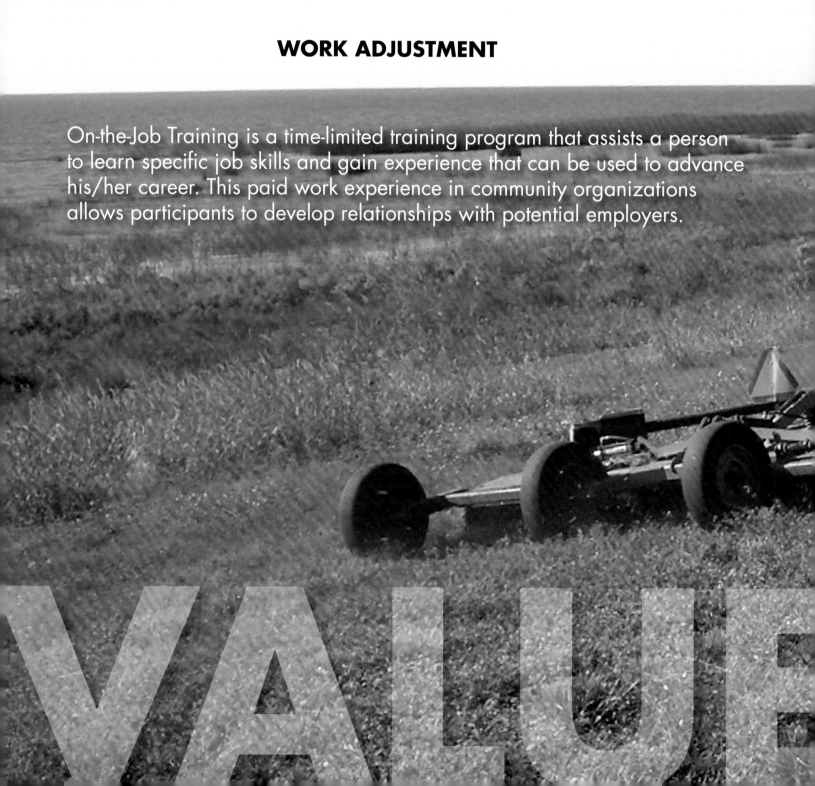

WORK ADJUSTMENT

On-the-Job Training is a time-limited training program that assists a person to learn specific job skills and gain experience that can be used to advance his/her career. This paid work experience in community organizations allows participants to develop relationships with potential employers.

VALUE

Opportunities abound in business and industry. We place individuals in a variety of jobs throughout the private and public sectors, and provide long-term assistance to ensure success.

SKILLS

Securing and maintaining competitive employment commensurate with the participant's interests, skills and abilities is the goal of Job Placement Services. Assisting individuals to locate employment leads, and to learn interviewing skills and résumé development are just some of the services our employment consultants provide. When necessary, job coaching and/or supported employment are available.

CONTRACT SERVICES

Training and supported employment opportunities are offered through Contact Services. The division provides individuals with opportunities to work for organizations in the community, such as Children's Medical Services, CVS Distribution Center, Department of Justice, Florida Department of Transportation, Health Care District of Palm Beach County, The Breakers Palm Beach, US Army Corps of Engineers and US Department of Agriculture.

TRAINING

SERVICE

South Florida's business is hospitality. The hospitality industry supports more than one million jobs for people in our community. Gulfstream Goodwill Industries has always maintained strong partnerships with local hotels and restaurants. This enables us to ensure continuous job placement for many of our participants in one of the biggest industries in South Florida.

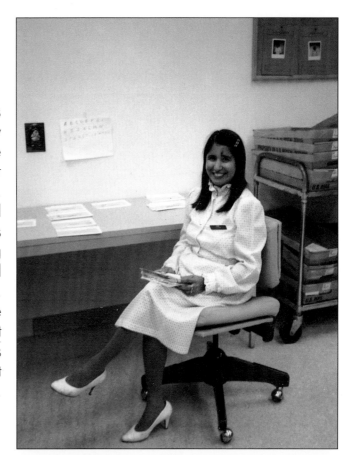

WORKERS' COMPENSATION

WORKERS' COMP WORKS FOR YOU

If you are injured on the job:

1. Notify your employer immediately to get the name of an approved physician. Workers' comp insurance may not pay the medical bills if you don't report your injury promptly to your employer.

2. Notify the doctor and medical staff that you were injured on the job so that bills may be properly filed.

3. If you have any problems with your claim or suffer excessive delays in treatment, contact the State of Florida's Division of Workers' Compensation at 1-800-342-1741.

Workers' Compensation pays for all authorized medically necessary care and treatment related to your injury or illness.

If you are unable to work or your earnings are lower because of a work related injury or illness, and you have been disabled for more than seven calendar days, you may be eligible for some wage replacement benefits.

$25,000 REWARD
ANTI-FRAUD REWARD PROGRAM

Rewards of up to $25,000 may be paid to persons providing information to the Department of Insurance leading to the arrest and conviction of persons committing insurance fraud, including employers who illegally fail to obtain workers' compensation coverage.

Persons may report suspected fraud to the department at 1-800-378-0445 or online at http://www.myfloridacfo.com/fraudpage.asp

A person is not subject to civil liability for furnishing such information, if such person acts without malice, fraud or bad faith.

This notice of Compliance must be posted by the employer and maintained conspicuously in and about the employer's place or places of employment. State of Florida Division of Workers' Compensation.

DFS-F4-1548
Revised March 2010

DO NOT REMOVE

1	21	41
2	22	42
3	23	43
4	24	44
5	25	45
6	26	46
7	27	47
8	28	48
9	29	49
10	30	50
11	31	51
12	32	52
13	33	53
14	34	54
15	35	55
16	36	56
17	37	57
18	38	58
19	39	59
20	40	60

Simplex

ATR120
ACROPRINT

11:03

Gulfstream Goodwill Industries inspires consumers and businesses to join us in having a positive impact on people and the planet. By donating goods, you help Goodwill divert millions of pounds of solid waste from landfills each year. The revenues from the collection and sale of these goods fund job training and placement programs right here in our community.

DONATE STUFF.
CREATE JOBS.
IMPROVE LIVES!

goodwill

Our donors make things happen. And their steadfast support fuels our passion for helping others. Most people don't realize that every piece of gently used clothing or household item donated turns into an opportunity for an individual to improve his or her life.

No one has ever become poor by giving.
Anne Frank

PASSION

ACTION

An information technology trainer instructs a group of Gulfstream Goodwill employees during new hire orientation.

50th ANNIVERSARY

THE TRAINING

Teaching a person particular skills or behaviors enables access to higher levels of functioning in all areas of life.

EVALUATION SERVICES

COMPREHENSIVE VOCATIONAL EVALUATION

Evaluation systematically uses work, real or simulated, as the focal point for the purpose of assisting individuals. The process is always tailored to an individual's needs and involves detailed interviewing to determine an assessment of academics, vocational interests, aptitudes, physical functioning, problem-solving and taking direction.

VOCATIONAL ASSESSMENT

This is an abbreviated assessment to determine performance in one or two skill areas. It may involve either assessment of academics and interests or a specific aptitude area the referring agent wishes to address.

Evaluation Services assesses and identifies the vocational skills, interests and abilities needed to be successful in the workplace. Through vocational and situational work activities designed to measure aptitude, clients gain self-confidence in decision making and work knowledge.

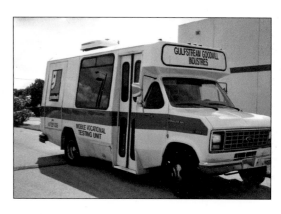

ON-THE-JOB EVALUATION

On-the-Job Evaluation provides realistic and detailed information regarding a participant's performance and work habits in a setting beyond traditional paper/pencil testing. A work trial is arranged in the community with an actual employer and a job coach is assigned to work with the individual to provide observations during the assessment period.

DISCOVERY

Participants are observed and interacted with in their homes and familiar environments in order to capture true skill sets. A vocational profile of the participant is generated as a result of the discovery process, moving the individual towards employment and identified supports needed to maintain such employment.

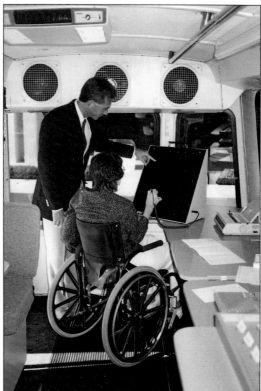

I don't want to live in the kind of world where we don't look out for each other. Not just the people that are close to us, but anybody who needs a helping hand. I can't change the way anybody else thinks, or what they choose to do, but I can do my bit.

Charles de Lint

Counselors work one-on-one with participants.

EMPLOYMENT SERVICES

Getting and keeping a job means understanding our strengths, desires, preferences and needs, while matching these qualities with the expectations of an employer.

The programs and services provided by Gulfstream Goodwill Industries that help individuals achieve employment success include direct job placement, community job connection, supported employment and benefits planning assistance.

Assisting individuals to locate employment leads, develop resumes and learn interviewing skills are just some of the services our employment consultants offer.

Some participants improve their skills through on-the-job training.

During National Disability Employment Awareness Month in October, Gulfstream Goodwill Industries recognizes community employers. Lowe's Store #0240 hired a former Goodwill participant who celebrated his one-year employment anniversary in 2015.

BRAIN INJURY SERVICES

Gulfstream Goodwill Industries' Headway Program for adults with brain injuries focuses on maximizing independence and community integration.

Lynee sustained a traumatic brain injury in a rollover accident. Unable to walk or do anything for herself, she spent months in a rehabilitation hospital. Upon release from the hospital, she was homeless and in need of help. After receiving initial support at the Women's Refuge in Vero Beach, Florida, Lynee was linked with a Gulfstream Goodwill Industries employment coach.

With hard work and determination, Lynee completed a nine-month work readiness program and was ready to re-enter a world of complete self-sufficiency. She secured a job as a polo horse groomer at a local farm. The owner of the farm saw great potential in Lynee and was moved by her inspirational attitude. "Lynee's life achievements since her accident are truly a gift to others who have come to know her," said employer Deborah Atwell.

From relearning how to perform simple tasks, such as tying one's shoes to cooking, to impulse control, the program works with individuals to improve independent living skills.

JUSTICE SERVICES

ADULT SERVICES

Re-Entry

In collaboration with Palm Beach County Public Safety, Palm Beach Sheriff's Office and Florida Department of Corrections, Gulfstream Goodwill Industries provides re-entry services to individuals who are returning home to Central Palm Beach County and the western communities from a period of incarceration.

YOUTH SERVICES

Good Leaders

A prevention program to keep at-risk youth from entering the justice system by teaching work readiness, leadership skills, decision-making skills and civic responsibility.

Back to a Future

The goal of this program is to reduce recidivism (reoffending), while connecting youth to employment, vocational/technical school or completion of a general education diploma (GED).

Alternatives to Secure Detention

This program provides monitoring, comprehensive case management, academic remediation, neuropsychological screening, testing and counseling to youth who are waiting for sentencing or on probation.

Barriers created by an individual's past can be overcome with tools and guidance to create a pathway to a new future. The program offers case management, evaluation, emergency services, referrals and job placement to help participants start a successful new life.

Staff and participants from the Offender Re-Entry Program attend the South Florida Fair.

Palm Beach County Main Courthouse

GOOD LEADERS GRADUATES

Don't follow the crowd, let the crowd follow you.
Margaret Thatcher

41

YOUTH FINDING THEIR WAY
BACK TO A FUTURE

We are made wise not by the recollection of our past,
but the responsibilty for our future.

George Bernard Shaw

Former NFL player and motivational speaker, Tyrus McCloud, speaks
to Back to a Future Program participants.

Adult Day Training (ADT) Program ("Transitions")

Transitions ADT Program is a day program for adults who have developmental disabilities. Gulfstream Goodwill Industries operates this program in West Palm Beach, Stuart, Ft. Pierce and Vero Beach. At these centers participants are taught job enhancement, personal growth, and health and wellness skills.

A Vero Beach Adult Day Training (ADT) Program case manager works with a patricipant. In the ADT Program, case managers work one-on-one with participants to improve employment, social and daily living skills.

In addition to an annual talent show, Adult Day Training (ADT) participants partake in a walk-a-thon every December. Staff begin walking with the participants three months before the event to build up their endurance and to get them excited about the event. These events go a long way in helping participants to build their self-confidence.

Honesty is about the scars. It's about the blemishes.
But it's more than just bragging about failure, which
could be a form of ego. It's about truly helping people.
James Altucher

NDEPENDENCE

DETERMINATION

A leader's job is not to do the work for others, it's to help others figure out how to do it themselves, to get things done, and to succeed beyond what they thought possible.

Simon Sinek

A Treasure Coast Adult Day Training (ADT) technician works with participants to build their computer skills during a regularly held technology training class.

*The purpose of life is ... to be useful, to be honorable,
to be compassionate, to have it make some difference that
you have lived and lived well.*
Ralph Waldo Emerson

An Adult Day Training (ADT) participant plays the Nintendo Wii™ at the Treasure Coast ADT center. The Wii™ is often used in rehabilitative settings, helping users to rebuild memory and cognitive skills and physical skills, such as balance and coordination.

50th ANNIVERSARY

THE EDUCATION

Education is crucial to the overall development of an individual and society at large. Knowledge about the world paves the way for a successful entry into the workforce, while building character and laying the foundation for a stronger community.

THE TRANSITION TO LIFE ACADEMY CHARTER SCHOOL

At the Transition to Life Academy charter school, students take classes to increase skills in specific areas to meet their personal goals. The students' academic performances are measured by applying teacher-developed and principal-approved academic assessment tools and successful employment outcomes.

The school serves students with disabilities, ages 18-21, who are seeking or have graduated with a special diploma and are transitioning from school to work.

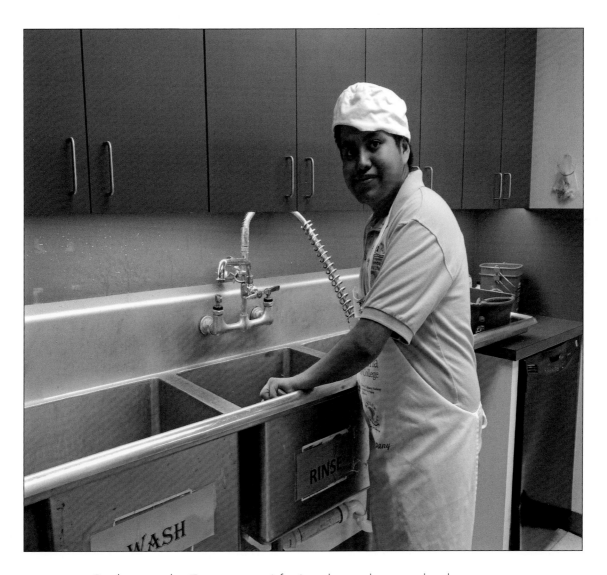

Students at the Transition to Life Academy charter school are provided with on-the-job training to increase their stamina and learn the soft skills necessary to maintain employment. A culinary career track teaches students the fundamental techniques through hands-on experience to be successful in the hospitality industry.

The charter school operates two special programs that link students with competitive job opportunities in a wide variety of fields: Project Search and High School High Tech.

Project Search enables students to gain work experience in a number of paid jobs in order to identify career goals.

High School High Tech provides exposure, education and experience to students with an interest in high-tech jobs and careers.

The Boca Resort & Club has been a long-standing partner of Gulfstream Goodwill's charter school in training and placing graduated students into jobs.

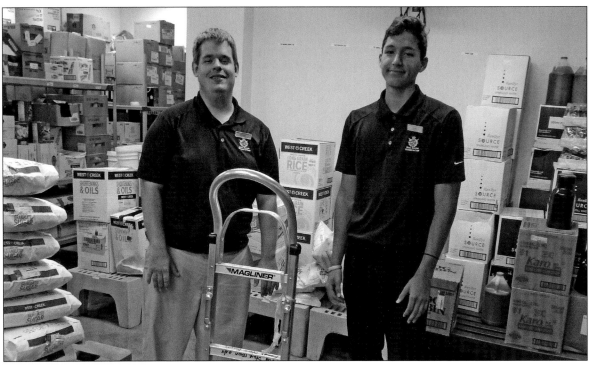

50th ANNIVERSARY

THE HOME

My day now begins and ends
with gratitude.

1000

Senator
Philip D. Lewis
Center

PALM BEACH COUNTY FLORIDA

Gulfstream Goodwill Industries has been providing homeless services since 1997 and took on the role of managing partner of the Senator Philip D. Lewis Homeless Resource Center in 2012. In its 50th year, Gulfstream Goodwill Industries is the largest provider of homeless services in Palm Beach County.

| | solid commitment 2015 Mayor's Ball Co-Chairs Pamela Goodman & Neil Schiller | Peg Ekberg | Rest in Peace Judge Wayne Andersen Judge Sheila O'Brien Mary & Maureen & Noreen | Jerry Daltorio and Bunny Daltorio | Arthur and Mary Lou Poisson | 2013 Community Partner of the Year Award Christ Fellowship | Pamela and Barky Goodman |

Karen and Paul Azahesa | Homeless Coalition Appreciates our AmeriCorps VISTA's | Tony Ralch | 2013 Business Spnsr. St. John The Evangelist Church | For Zarley & Ziggy Aigen, Love Nana & Grandpa Aigen-Scott | 2013 Hero Sponsor Palm Beach Aggregates | AKPsi - Sigma On Shaping People Shaping Busine

Thank you Phil for all you did! Gleason Stambaugh Jr | Emily Kimmel | Betzy & Michael Rega | Hyacinthia Becton Together we can give help in time of need | Alpha Kappa Psi Fraternity - Florida Atlantic University | Mary Kay Murray | Ken Gamelin & Assoc. Insurance & Invstmts (561) 588-5030 | VA

In Memory of Phil Lewis Frances M. Stambaugh | 2013 Business Spnsr. Southern Waste Systems | The Lindskoog Family Jeff Cindy Dawn Dustin Kaiden | Renee Constantino Georgiana Devine Carol Shaffer | Thank You Phil Lewis Rest in Peace Judge Katie Kearney | Salvation Army United Way PBC YWCA | "Come Holy S Fr. Ted Hesb by Diana Le

Thank you Senator Phil Lewis for your leadership | John Clark Putting faith into action | In Memory of Don & Betty Ion | Operation Hope PBC Community Svcs. PBC Div. Human Svcs. | Church of God CILO Community Caring Ctr | FEC Farmworker Coordinating Council | Ctr. for Family Svcs. Children's Home Scty Children's Svcs Cncl

Lewis Luncheon er Hero 2014 PNC | Hannah and Hunter Stone | 211 Adopt-A-Family AVDA | Paul Gionfriddo William Graham Susan Darby Guillama | David Gury Shannon Sadler Hull Stephen Johnson | Robert Anis Scott Badesch Thomas Bell | NOAH Housing Leadership Council

Homes of da 2015 | deboss | 2013 Business Spnsr. The Benz Family Trust. | | | ten2end | Jack Scarola Andrew Sherman William Washington | Oakwood Center PB Assisted Living Facility

ponsor of s Center otorcars | The choices we make dictate the lives we lead (L&J Glucksman) | SCMH Stand Down House The Lord's Place | Suzette Werner Ron Wieword Steve Wilson | ten2end | TheHomelessPlan.org Palm Beach County Homeless Advisory Board "It starts today!" | Jeffery Lindskoog Mariam Maldonado Jean Malecki | Community Foundation CARP

lewis ll you Family | John Raich | Taylor and Thad IV Lewis | | Thomas Masters Bill Oberlink Nancy Perez | | |

In Appreciation of Marilyn Munoz | In Memory of Peter Scott Sherman | Business Sponsor 2013 Carlos Morrison | PBC Health Dpt. PBC Sheriff's Office School District PBC | John F. Koons, Chair Leo Abdella Judith Aigen | Palm Beach County Board of County Commissioners | Claudia Tuck Jon Van Arnam |

Pamela Goodman Thank you for your leadership | | | Robert Kellman Ezra Krieg Philip Lewis | Rita Ellis Lois Frankel Kerry Gallagher | Don Chester MichelleDiffenderfer Gaetana Ebbole | Perry Borman Jorge Camejo Michele Carte

ss Spnsr. nvironmental ervices | 2013 Business Spnsr. Palm Beach Kennel Club | Legal Aid Society Homeless Coalition of Palm Beach County | Be Extraordinary India Howley | DCF Gulfstream Goodwill Housing Partnership | |

The Senator Philip D. Lewis Center

As Palm Beach County's central point of entrance for homeless individuals to receive services, the center offers referral, intake, assessment, medical services, shelter beds, vocational placement and life skills training. Services are offered in partnership with Palm Beach County Human Services, Homeless Coalition of Palm Beach County, the Palm Beach County Health Department, Adopt-A-Family, The Lord's Place and homeless service providers in the Palm Beach County Homeless and Housing Alliance Program (formerly the Continuum of Care).

It's not enough to have lived. We should be determined to live for something. May I suggest that it be creating joy for others, sharing what we have for the betterment of personkind, bringing hope to the lost and love to the lonely.

Leo Buscaglia

Project Success, Project Succeed, Beacon Place and New Avenues

Through the US Department of Housing and Urban Development, Gulfstream Goodwill Industries offers rent assistance programs and long-term support services to enable persons with disabilities, who were formerly homeless, to maintain their own apartments in the community. Apartments are located in eastern and western Palm Beach County communities.

Beacon Place residents and Residential Services staff.

Home at J Street

"Home at J Street", owned and operated by Gulfstream Goodwill, offers long-term supportive, affordable housing in four buildings for people who are transitioning out of homelessness.

Before

50th ANNIVERSARY

THE SIGHT & SOUND

To evolve and adapt are the essence of being human. Strength does not come from physical capacity. It lies in an individual's determination to succeed.

The Lighthouse, established in 1946, was originally located on Dixie Highway in West Palm Beach and called Lions Industries. The name was changed to Lighthouse for the Blind of the Palm Beaches in 1978. In 2008, Lighthouse for the Blind merged with Gulfstream Goodwill Industries and moved its offices into its current location just off of 45th Street in West Palm Beach.

Vision Services/ Lighthouse for the Blind of the Palm Beaches

Services are available to those who are blind or have low vision. They are provided by staff certified in how to accomplish the many tasks of daily living, orientation and mobility and how to use computers with the latest adaptive technology. A low vision doctor evaluates participants, and prescribes optical aides and provides training in their use. A social worker conducts intake for Lighthouse services and makes referrals to community resources. The Lighthouse also stocks and sells products for nonvisual adaptions and low vision use.

Commonly confused with other organizations that include the word "lighthouse" in their names, Lighthouse for the Blind of the Palm Beaches is the only organization of its kind based in West Palm Beach, FL, and serving Palm Beach, Martin, St. Lucie, Indian River and Okeechobee Counties.

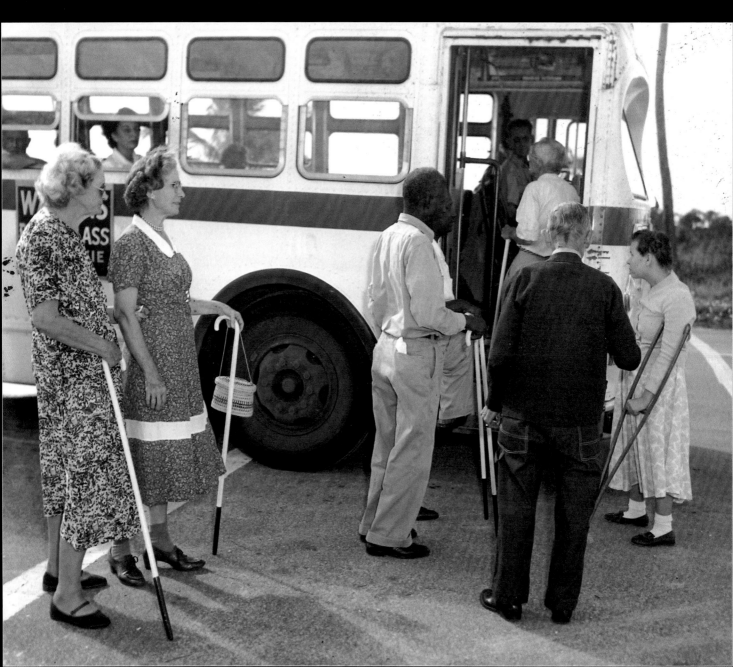

Visually impaired participants have traditionally used public transportation to come to the Lighthouse to receive services. Most visually impaired individuals carry white canes, which are used as mobility tools and as a means of self-sufficiency.

The Learning Independence through Experience (LITE) Club is a year-round program offered by the Lighthouse for the Blind of the Palm Beaches for youth in kindergarten through 12th grade. The program provides quality services for children who are blind or visually impaired.

A Lighthouse participant learns to use assistive technology to communicate with others.

INDEPENDENT LIVING SKILLS

Through Independent Living Skills Training at the Lighthouse, participants learn personal management (time telling, money identification), home management (oven and stove safety, sewing) and communications skills (dialing the phone, Braille).

An independent living instructor teaches participants to decipher information on canned food labels with assistive technology.

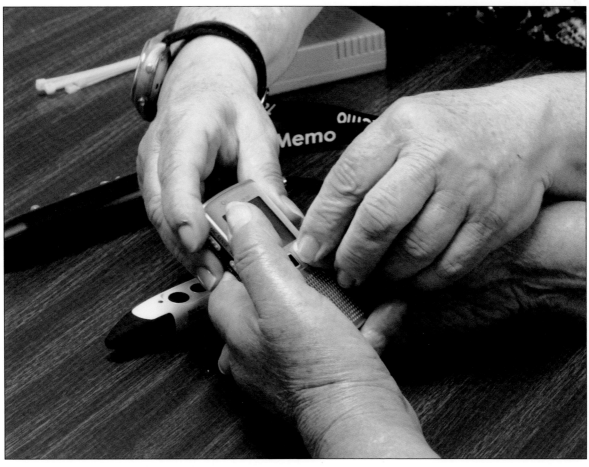

INSPIRATION

Fundraising events, charitable donations
and community support are important sources of income
for the Lighthouse.

Every March, the Lighthouse for the Blind is the honored beneficiary
of the Music for the Mind Concert Series, an opportunity made
possible thanks to the Kretzer Piano Music Foundation. This annual
fundraiser is held at the Harriet Himmel Theatre in City Place and
features the music of blind pianist David Crohan.

FISHING TOURNAMENT

The Lighthouse for the Blind of the Palm Beaches has closed its annual events season with the Lighthouse Ladies KDW (kingfish, dolphin, wahoo) Fishing tournament since 2011. The tournament is generously hosted by Debbie and Ray Lorenzo of Stingray Fishing Outfitters, who believe in the organization's mission. More than 150 lady anglers compete in the annual tournament, which culminates with an exciting awards ceremony in the north end of Palm Beach County.

DEAF SERVICES

With more than 200,000 people with some degree of hearing loss in Palm Beach County alone, Gulfstream Goodwill Industries provides the resources necessary for these individuals to better connect within their communities.

Staff with experience in deaf culture and who are fluent in American Sign Language provide advocacy; interpretation; job placement; resume writing; crisis intervention; and assistance applying for social services, such as food stamps and health insurance. Deaf Services provides equal access to all programs offered by Gulfstream Goodwill for the Deaf in our community.

Community outreach and education are another major component of Deaf Services. Staff educates the community about the American with Disabilities Act (ADA) and how to provide equal access to information and communication with the Deaf. We help employers, agencies, medical and other service providers understand when and how to provide an interpreter, and how to receive tax credits for provisions that are made to ensure compliance with ADA law.

50th ANNIVERSARY

THE SUPPORT SYSTEM

Gulfstream Goodwill Industries retail thrift stores are the backbone of the organization. They're what keeps the lights on so we're able to offer all our health, human and social services programs to the community.

RETAIL OPERATIONS

PROGRESS

Participants in the West Palm Beach Adult Day Training (ADT) Program create original pieces of art each year to be auctioned off to raise funds for their program activities. Selected participant artwork from the auctions was integrated into the exterior architecture of Gulfstream Goodwill's Gatlin Store in Port St. Lucie.

SUCCESS

The best antidote I know for worry is work. The best cure for weariness is the challenge of helping someone who is even more tired. One of the great ironies of life is this: He or she who serves almost always benefits more than he or she who is served.

Gordon B. Hinckley

EXCELLENCE

The fifteenth retail store operated by Gulfstream Goodwill Industries opened its doors in 2001. As of its 50th anniversary, 28 stores are fully operational throughout Palm Beach, Martin, St. Lucie, Indian River and Okeechobee Counties.

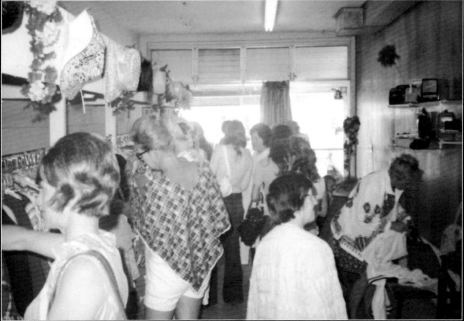

... NOW

BOCA RATON BOUTIQUE

Gulfstream Goodwill Industries' boutique shops showcase the very best its retail stores have to offer. The organization has four boutique stores and a vintage shoppe in Boca Raton, Palm Beach, Palm Beach Gardens and Wellington.

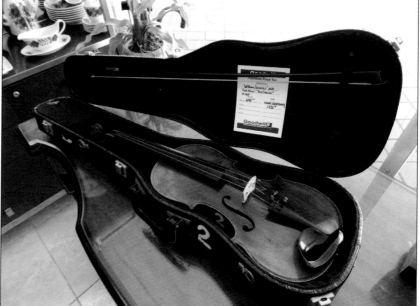

NORTHLAKE BOUTIQUE & VINTAGE SHOPPE

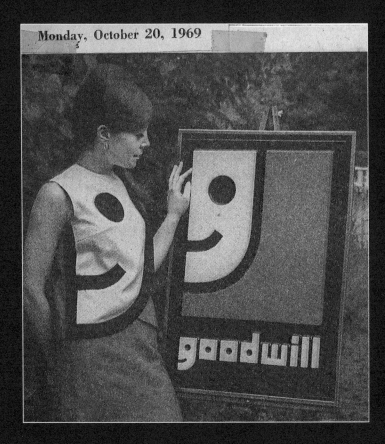

Pauline de Pasquale, wearing a mod version of the colorful Goodwill Industries symbol, poses by the smiling letter 'G' that represents a rehabilitated individual, as well as Goodwill.

Whether a rehabilitated program participant or a friendly professional chosen out of the local community to join our team, Gulfstream Goodwill represents many smiling faces.

THEN ...

... NOW

Gulfstream Goodwill Industries' network administrator installs the organization's new Point of Sale (POS) systems at the Stuart Store in 2015. (Below) One of the agency's first cash registers.

GIVE CHANGE TO
MAKE A
CHANGE
GULFSTREAM GOODWILL
PUTS PEOPLE TO WORK!

DA EL CAMBIO
PARA HACER UN CAMBIO

GULFSTREAM GOODWILL
PONE A LA GENTE A TRABAJAR

Traumatic Brain Injury Program

114

Customers are asked to contribute to Gulfstream Goodwill Industries by doing more than simply shopping. Shoppers are asked to donate the change from their purchases a part of the organization's Give Change to Make a Change Campaign. Proceeds are used to support Gulfstream Goodwill's programs and services.

Here are the values that I stand for: honesty, equality, kindness, compassion, treating people the way you want to be treated and helping those in need. To me, those are traditional values.

Ellen DeGeneres

"GREEN" OPERATIONS

REUSE
REDUCE
RECYCLE

A salvage worker places donated clothing into a baler at the North Operations Warehouse in Fort Pierce.

Bales of clothing are prepared to go through Gulfstream Goodwill Industries salvage program. When clothes have rotated through retail stores without being sold, many times due to seasonal demands, the clothes are sold to overseas markets. This ensures that revenue is generated from every piece of donated clothing received by the agency. The salvage effort is also part of the agency's green initiative to divert clothing and other items from landfills.

RECYCLING

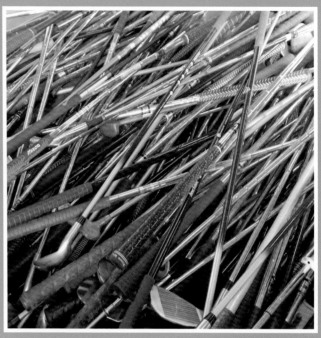

With retail operations covering a five-county area, transportation is essential.
Gulfstream Goodwill Industries has always used a variety of vehicles to transport donated goods to,
from and within donation centers, retail stores and warehouses.

THEN ...

... NOW

CONFIDENCE

The E-Books program sells used books through Alibris, Amazon, eBay and Half.com.

Dell Reconnect

Gulfstream Goodwill Industries stepped into the E-Commerce market in 2010.

The Good Geeks Computer Refurbishing Department sells quality refurbished desktop and laptop computers, printers, keyboards, routers, modems, ink and toner cartridges, mobile GPS units, iPhones, and vintage audio and video components through eBay. Good Geeks also provides skills training to program participants.